MELODIE ANDERSON

# Am I an Alcoholic?
*IDENTIFYING SIGNS OF ALCOHOLISM*

Copyright © 2023 by Melodie Anderson

All rights reserved. No part of this publication may be reproduced, stored or transmitted in any form or by any means, electronic, mechanical, photocopying, recording, scanning, or otherwise without written permission from the publisher. It is illegal to copy this book, post it to a website, or distribute it by any other means without permission.

Melodie Anderson asserts the moral right to be identified as the author of this work.

Melodie Anderson has no responsibility for the persistence or accuracy of URLs for external or third-party Internet Websites referred to in this publication and does not guarantee that any content on such Websites is, or will remain, accurate or appropriate.

Designations used by companies to distinguish their products are often claimed as trademarks. All brand names and product names used in this book and on its cover are trade names, service marks, trademarks and registered trademarks of their respective owners. The publishers and the book are not associated with any product or vendor mentioned in this book. None of the companies referenced within the book have endorsed the book.

First edition

This book was professionally typeset on Reedsy.
Find out more at reedsy.com

# Contents

| | | |
|---|---|---|
| 1 | INTRODUCTION | 1 |
| 2 | DEFINITION OF AN ALCOHOLIC | 3 |
| 3 | PHYSICAL AND BEHAVIORAL SIGNS | 5 |
| 4 | GENETIC FACTORS | 7 |
| 5 | THE STAGES OF ALCOHOLISM | 9 |
| 6 | HEALTH CONSEQUENCES | 11 |
| 7 | MENTAL HEALTH EFFECTS | 13 |
| 8 | IMPACTS ON RELATIONSHIPS | 17 |
| 9 | RECOVERY OPTIONS | 21 |
| 10 | OUTPATIENT TREATMENT | 24 |
| 11 | INPATIENT TREATMENT | 25 |
| 12 | ONLINE SUPPORT COMMUNITIES | 26 |
| 13 | BOOKS AND RECOMMENDED READING | 28 |
| 14 | WHAT IS DETOXIFICATION? | 31 |
| 15 | 12 STEP PROGRAMS | 32 |
| 16 | SETTING RECOVERY GOALS | 34 |
| 17 | BUILDING A SUPPORT SYSTEM | 37 |
| 18 | BIBLE STUDY GROUPS | 39 |
| 19 | CONCLUSION | 40 |
| 20 | RESOURCES | 41 |
| | *About the Author* | 42 |

# 1

# INTRODUCTION

**Welcome**

Hi, my name is Melodie Anderson and I am happy to share with you my experience in determining whether or not you are truly an alcoholic.

**Introduction**

I am a 64 yr old woman living in Brentwood, Tennessee. My greatest blessings are having four grown children, three daughters and my son. Who have now blessed me with 8 grandchildren with the 9th one due in December 2023.

It was about 4 years ago that I too questioned whether or not I was an alcoholic. The last thing I wanted was to be defined by the phrase "I am an alcoholic" I wasn't living under a bridge and I hadn't lost my home or my job. I still worked everyday, I didn't hide my alcohol in a paper bag. What I did do was I planned out which liquor store to go to, I couldn't face the employees two days in a row, so I rotated a few stores. I would wake up every morning with a splitting headache vowing I wasn't drinking that day. But around one o'clock I would start planning where and when I could go buy some. It felt like my skin was crawling waiting to get off work. I would call people at night while drinking and not remember a single word I said the next morning. I would visit family and not want to drink in front of them more than the one drink offered, but instead of enjoying myself I was edging out the door to get back to my friend, alcohol. It had become my master and best friend and I was isolating every night with a bottle. I drank seven days a week and towards the end I started drinking in the early mornings of the weekends. It was only a matter of time before I started drinking before work. I totaled two vehicles. I quit accepting invitations with friends. I was all alone hiding from the world with my friend, alcohol. It was a miserable existence. I found myself packing bottles of wine in my suitcase to go and visit my children in their homes because I knew the one glass they offered me would never fulfill the cravings inside me. So I would go to bed early and drink in my room and sneak the bottles out when they were not home. It was a miserable existence.

# 2

# DEFINITION OF AN ALCOHOLIC

Let me share with you what I learned and what worked for my recovery.
**DEFINITION OF AN ALCOHOLIC**

*Alcoholic Anonymous defines it as a physical compulsion, coupled with a mental obsession to consume alcohol,"* in which cravings for alcohol are always catered to, even at times when they should not be.

Alcoholism is having the **inability** to control drinking due to both a physical and emotional dependence on alcohol.
Symptoms usually include a strong need or urge to drink alcohol. Those with alcohol use disorder may have problems controlling their drinking, some say "we don't have an off switch" we continue to use alcohol even though it is causing problems for us and our relationships, or have withdrawal symptoms when you decrease your usual amount or even stop drinking.

People will say to you "Don't you have the willpower to stop?" It wasn't a matter of my will. It was a physical compulsion. I needed it as much as I wanted it. It is a chronic disease of the brain that can happen to anyone.

**Most of us never tell the Dr. how many drinks we actually have every week.**
Alcoholics generally drink excessively, often more than four drinks a day and in a manner that they cannot control. Excessive drinking is a serious health problem for millions of people in the United States. Heavy drinking and binge drinking are not necessarily an addiction, but both of these conditions increase risk of becoming dependent on, and addicted to, alcohol.

# 3

# PHYSICAL AND BEHAVIORAL SIGNS

- Nausea and vomiting
- Headaches
- Abdominal Pain
- High temperature and/or chills
- The "shakes"
- A strong need or urge to use alcohol
- Problems controlling alcohol
- Continue to use alcohol even though it is causing problems
- Withdrawal symptoms when stopping or decreasing alcohol
- Blackouts
- Dizziness
- Shakiness
- Craving
- Sweating
- Aggression
- Agitation

- Compulsive behavior
- Self-destructive behavior
- Lack of restraint
- Delirium or fear
- Physical substance dependence
- Problems with coordination
- Slurred speech
- Tremors
- Going to jail a lot
- Suicidal thoughts

# 4

# GENETIC FACTORS

Alcohol abuse often runs in the family. We hear about scientific studies of an "alcoholic gene." Research also shows that genes are only responsible for half of the risk of alcohol abuse. Why do some members of the family become addicted while others don't?

The biggest risk factors are having a biological family member with alcoholism or drug addiction. Having a mental health condition such as bipolar disorder, depression or anxiety. Experiencing peer pressure to drink. Having low self-esteem or self-worth. Family plays the biggest role in a person's likelihood of developing alcoholism. Children who are exposed to alcohol abuse from an early age are more at risk of falling into a dangerous drinking pattern. Starting college or a new job can also make you more susceptible to the peer pressure of drinking.

There are genes that increase a person's risk, as well as those that may decrease that risk. For instance, some people of Asian descent carry a gene variant that alters their rate of alcohol metabolism, causing them to have symptoms like flushing, nausea, and rapid heartbeat when they drink. Many people who have these effects avoid alcohol, which helps

protect them from developing a drinking disorder.
Scientists are always exploring how genes may influence the effectiveness of treatments for Alcohol abuse. For instance some doctors recommend naltrexone because it has shown to help some, but not all, patients with a drinking disorder who have a variation of a specific gene respond positively to treatment with the drug. While those without the specific gene do not respond with the drug. A fuller understanding of how genes influence treatment outcomes will help doctors prescribe the treatment that is most likely to help each patient.
National Institute on Alcohol Abuse and Alcoholism

# 5

# THE STAGES OF ALCOHOLISM

**First stage**: You have the prehistoric alcoholic who shows very little signs of abuse. The first involves experimentation with alcohol and it is when alcohol tolerance develops as you begin to drink regularly as a coping mechanism for stress, anxiety or other emotions.

**Second stage:** It is when the development of a pattern starts.Drinking becomes more regular, and people find themselves to begin using social gatherings as excuses to drink. They also may start using negative consequences in their life as an excuse to drink. "I've had a bad day" "I've had a fight with my spouse" "You would if you were going through what I am going through" "I deserve this after my work schedule." Also the negative consequences of drinking such as hangovers can cause us to drink because of it.

**Third stage:** This is the most crucial stage. It is when a person starts drinking frequently and consistently, maybe even starting their day off with a drink. They may struggle with their friend and family relationships. They may experience changes to their behavior that impacts their lives negatively. They also may start experiencing health issues such as hangovers, blackouts and feeling sick more often than when not drinking.

**Late stage:** The final stage leads to a complete loss of control over alcohol. This stage is where you feel as if you **MUST** drink. At this point your body begins to require you to drink just to feel normal, this is known as dependence. You may find that if you don't drink you start experiencing withdrawal symptoms and intense cravings.

# 6

# HEALTH CONSEQUENCES

High blood pressure, heart disease and digestive problems. Cancer of the breast, mouth, throat, esophagus, voice box, liver, colon and rectum. Weakening of the immune system, increasing the chances of getting sick. Learning and memory problems, including dementia and poor school performance.
Long term effects of frequently drinking can include: persistent changes in mood, including anxiety, insomnia and other sleep issues. A weakened immune system, meaning you may get sick more often.

Symptoms of alcohol abuse to your body include mental confusion, difficulty remaining conscious, vomiting, seizures, trouble breathing, slow heart rate, clammy skin, dulled responses (such as no gag reflex which prevents choking), extremely low body temperature. Alcohol abuse can lead to brain damage or death.

Alcohol interferes with your brain's communication pathways and can affect the way your brain functions. Alcohol makes it harder for the brain areas such as controlling balance, memory, speech and judgment to do your job. Usually resulting in a higher likelihood of injuries and other negative outcomes.

I had also developed a rash of sores on my body that would not go away. Numerous doctors visits told me they were chigger bites. They were everywhere and no medication worked. My immune system was so weakened.

The first signs of liver damage are:

- Feeling sick
- Weight loss
- Loss of appetite
- Yellowing of the eyes and skin
- Swelling in the ankles and stomach
- Confusion or drowsiness
- Vomiting blood or passing blood in your stools http://www.healthline.com

# 7

# MENTAL HEALTH EFFECTS

Alcohol affects the part of the brain that controls inhibition, so you may feel more relaxed, less anxious and more confident after a drink. We all want that right? But what happens when it wears off? The chemical changes in your brain can soon lead to more negative feelings, such as anger, depression or anxiety, regardless of what mood you're in.
Mentalhealth.org

The damage that is done to your central nervous system can vary dramatically depending on how much you consume, what your weight is and your bodily make-up. Symptoms of alcohol intoxication, such as mild cognitive and physical impairment, may become evident after just one or two drinks. But heavier use can result in alcohol overdose or can be alcohol poisoning if consumed too much during one sitting. Alcohol poisoning is a dangerous and potentially deadly consequence of drinking large amounts in a short amount of time.
Alcohol poisoning symptoms may include:

- Confusion
- Seizure
- Problems trying to stay conscience
- Respiratory troubles
- Heart rate decreasing
- Vomiting
- Permanent cognitive disruption or impairment
- In the worst case, death

Studies have shown that there is more brain shrinkage in those who consume large quantities over time.

**For a mental health professional to diagnose someone with an alcohol abuse disorder, a person must meet at least two of the following criteria within a 12-month span.**

**Lets see how many you have, I know I sure had a lot of them.**

- **Spending a significant amount of time trying to obtain alcohol.**
- **Experiencing cravings for alcohol.**
- **Drinking while in situations where it is dangerous to do so, such as while driving or operating machinery**
- **Continuing to drink in spite of familial and relationship issues caused by your drinking.**
- **Being unable to fulfill obligations at work, home or school because of alcohol use.**
- **Using higher or more frequent amounts of alcohol than originally intended.**
- **Tolerance, or needing higher amounts of alcohol to achieve previ-**

ous effects.
- Being unable to cut down on drinking.
- Continuing to drink despite negative physical or mental health consequences.
- Avoiding activities that you once enjoyed so you can drink.
- Experience alcohol withdrawal symptoms if you try to stop drinking.
- Drinking alone or in secret
- Increased tolerance to alcohol

Here are some interesting statistics I found.

**ALCOHOL CONSUMPTION IN THE U.S.**

Alcohol is considered socially acceptable in the United States and many Americans consume alcohol on a regular basis. Drinking too much, however, can be very harmful to your health. Between 2011 and 2015, alcohol abuse was responsible for roughly 95,000 deaths, and excessive alcohol use caused the death of 1 in 10 adults between the ages of 20 and 64.

The 2018 National survey on Drug use and Health reports that 139.8 million Americans aged 12 or older currently drink alcohol, 67.1 million were considered binge drinkers, and 16.6 million were classified as heavy drinkers. The NIAAA defines binge drinking as consuming enough alcohol to raise your BAC to 0.8 g/dl in a single occasion. This generally translates to 4 drinks for women and 5 for men within a 2 hour period.<u>American Addiction Centers: Resources for Addiction Rehabilitation</u>

# 8

# IMPACTS ON RELATIONSHIPS

If our partner or loved one is regularly drinking more than we are, it can have an impact on our own feelings, creating tension and anxiety. For example, we may feel that we take second place to our loved one's drinking, or that they are increasingly physically and emotionally absent.

How do alcoholics behave in a relationship?
Verbal abuse under the influence, cheating, financial infidelity, lying, and other common choices of alcoholics may be defining factors of your life as well as your relationship. You are missing out on having a relationship with someone who cares about you and or your well-being as much as you care about them.

Alcohol abuse is one of the leading addictions many people face. Not only can alcohol wreak havoc on someone's personal life, but it also greatly affects every single relationship they are a part of. Perhaps the biggest and most detrimental impacts come at the level of intimacy, partnership and marriage.

Anyone who is engaging in heavy drinking on a regular basis will be faced with many emotional, physical, and psychological challenges, which tend to be most fully expressed inside of their closest relationships. People with an alcohol problem usually have a very hard time maintaining healthy relationships because of their alcohol intake.

The effect of alcoholism on relationships and intimacy is widespread and touches on many different areas of intimate affairs.

**How does alcoholism affect intimacy and sex?**

Alcoholism's effects on relationships can be quite harmful. The first area that is usually affected is intimacy, which doesn't always mean sex, either. Parts of an intimate relationship that can be affected by the effects of alcoholism include:

- Trust
- Stability
- Affection
- Expectations
- Commitment
- Shared values
- Respect

When alcohol is involved this raises concern for codependency probabilities as well as abusive behavior both verbally and physically.

Deterioration in married or unmarried couples often stems from arguments, financial troubles, acts of infidelity or, worse, domestic violence.

Most people are left asking can my relationship survive alcoholism? There is evidence that a relationship can make it, but some would argue that it won't. For the married population with one person being the heavy drinker, research shows that 50% are more likely to end in divorce according to a study on Medical Daily

### How alcohol abuse impacts your sex drive

Alcohol abuse, over time, will most likely result in a lack of sexual functioning in both men and women. As a person becomes more addicted, they tend to lose interest in sex or being close with someone as their abuse becomes the number one priority in their life. Alcohol abuse in males is known to create difficulty in becoming or staying aroused often resulting in erectile dysfunction. Women have been known to suffer from a decreased libido from alcohol use disorder also.

For people outside of a committed relationship, alcohol can lead to unplanned pregnancy and sexually transmitted disease due to having sex while under the influence.

According to a study reported by NETDOCTOR, research suggests that sexual promiscuity as a result of alcohol is definitely something to consider for people who are not in a committed relationship. The study found:

- Alcohol was a major factor in persuading men and women to have unsafe sex without the use of a condom.
- Seventy percent of people who regretted having a sexual encounter stated that alcohol had been the influence that made their decision.
- When young people were surveyed, ten percent said they had been so intoxicated that they couldn't remember whether they had sex or not.
- Of that group of young adults, 28 percent said they had sex with someone they wouldn't normally be attracted to mostly due to alcohol - often referred to as "beer goggles"

# 9

# RECOVERY OPTIONS

So you think you may be an alcoholic or you know someone who might be. The good news is there is help in many ways and many treatment options. Keep in mind you cannot save anyone from their alcoholism. They must want to get help on their own.

When faced with alcoholism in a relationship seeking treatment may be the best option. Treatment can help the person with the drinking problem begin recovery and start living a healthier life.
In treatment therapy is encouraged for both people involved as they work to rebuild their relationship. Usually individual counseling, as well as group counseling or family counseling, is part of the treatment for alcohol abuse.
Partners and spouses should seek personal counseling and a supportive community with others who understand what they may be experiencing. This can help to restore peace and balance as you support your partner through their recovery.

The first step for treatment of alcoholism is DETOXIFICATION. It is the initial step in treating alcoholism, and it can also be the most difficult. Within the first few days after you quit drinking, you may experience extremely uncomfortable withdrawal symptoms. Because of this, the alcohol detox stage should be completed under professional care.

- Medical Detox which safely rids your body of toxins and substances while alleviating withdrawal symptoms under medical supervision.

- Residential Treatment will be a supportive, home-like setting with intensive therapy and 24-hour supervision.

- Partial Hospitalization is structured to provide a day time program intensive therapy and skill building groups at their facilities.

Intensive Outpatient is a step down from the higher levels of care. It's called IOP and it offers structure and support to maintain recovery
Some facilities provide all four of these.
Again, it will depend on if your insurance covers whichever facility you chose.

Recovery Houses do not usually care if you have insurance or not. They just charge a weekly fee and require you to work during the day. There are non christian ones and christian ones. The christian ones usually want you to attend church services a few times a week. This is the one I chose. I attended church a few times a week, I heard a saying that God brought me to the facility and the program led me right back to God. My relationship with God grew at a rate I never thought was possible. The closer I grew to God the easier my program of recovery was. The quicker my relationships healed with my family. The healing of my body and soul was so miraculous. I cried and fell to my knees in church because I could actually feel again. I thank God everyday for healing me. I now live a life of total dependance on God and I am 4 years sober and the happiest I have ever been. My mind is clear, my conscience is clean. I have money in my pocket instead of blowing it on alcohol. My grandchildren ride in the car with me and my own children have the peace of mind that I am sober. I am clear headed I can function in society and I actually enjoy going out with friends. Some friends and family still drink and I will have a tonic water with lime with them. They don't mind and I still laugh and have a blast. It no longer occurs to me to have alcohol. It took me over a year to really feel this way.

The first week is the hardest

Try not to allow yourself to get bored

Staying busy is key

I found that I had so much extra free time in my thinking and in my day to day activities. You don't realize how much time and energy went into thinking of it, planning it, getting it, hiding and drinking it.

# 10

## OUTPATIENT TREATMENT

Quitting alcohol and certain drugs suddenly, or "cold turkey" is dangerous, even fatal. Intensive Outpatient Treatment also known as (IOP)allows you the freedom to engage in the world around you while in a safe, supportive therapeutic setting. During outpatient treatment you participate in a four-day, 12-hour weekly therapy program with individual therapy sessions each week.

Some facilities provide Partial Hospitalization Programs where you live in center housing while participating in an ongoing customized treatment plan. This option is different from inpatient Treatment Centers as it allows you to have your

# 11

## INPATIENT TREATMENT

There are many to choose from. The first thing I would do is google "treatment facilities near me" unless you want to choose a luxury one than google " top treatment facilities for alcoholism". Obviously the top luxury ones will have to qualify you through your insurance.

There are many recovery houses that just charge you a weekly fee. I've heard it's between $200-300 a week. You must work at the Recovery houses. They won't let you sit around.

If you go to a treatment center some will offer:

Your own vehicle and technology. This program is helpful for people who are transitioning out of residential care or who don't have a safe place to live while they continue their treatment.

I do believe that Outpatient Treatment Centers need your insurance too.

# 12

# ONLINE SUPPORT COMMUNITIES

Finding support when facing addiction can be overwhelming. Here are some of the best support groups that might help.

It feels as if alcohol is everywhere in today's culture. No matter where I look, you seem to see ads enticing you with the promise of how much more fun your life can be with a few more drinks. But for someone working on their sobriety, these ads are far from fun reminders of our addiction.

Still, recovery from alcohol and substance abuse is possible, especially if you have a good support system.online sobriety and alcohol recovery groups can help you navigate your journey to getting better. Online groups are usually free although some accept donations.

Here is a list of the best reported Online Support Groups

- Best Overall: Alcoholics Anonymous, it's free, it offers in-person and online support.

- Best Online Toolkit: SMART Recovery
- Best Secular community: LifeRing
- Best Support Group for women: Women for Sobriety
- Best Social media app: Sober Grid
- Best for a sober lifestyle and its an App: Loosid
- Best for Mindfulness: Club Soda (yes that's a program) it is free but they do offer courses starting at about $50.
- Best Group coaching Program: Tempest, this one is not free, it starts at $59 a month: coaching starts at $199 for (four sessions) but you get one on one coaching.

What online support groups have done for me is to know there are others out there living with similar issues and that there is hope for recovery. These groups provide the members an outlet to share both wins and losses that they may not feel comfortable sharing with anyone else. Studies

# 13

# BOOKS AND RECOMMENDED READING

My personal favorite is: **Living Sober** by Anonymous
It's a book about helping get over those urges, low self esteem and more. It allowed me to speak about my feelings about what was going on with me. Week to week you will notice as people get sober, they will begin to express their progress and begin to understand the journey that they are on in a very positive way.

Biographies, Memoirs, & 'Quit Lit'

- A Happier Hour by Rebecca Weller
- Between Breaths: A Memoir of Panic and Addiction by Elizabeth Vargas
- Punch Me to the Gods by Brian Broome

BOOKS AND RECOMMENDED READING

- Nothing Good can come from this by Kristi Coulter
- The Unexpected Joy of being Sober by Catherine Gray
- We are the luckiest: The Surprising Magic of Being Sober by Laura McKowen
- The Sober Diaries by Clare Pooley
- Healing Neen: One Woman's Path to Salvation from Trauma and Addiction by Tonier Cain
- Blackout: Remembering the Things I Drank to Forget by Sarah Hepola
- Drinking: A Love Story by Caroline Knapp

Best Non-Fiction Books About Alcohol and Recovery

- Quit Like a Woman by Holly Whitaker
- Drink: The Intimate Relationship Between Women and Alcohol by Ann Dowsett Johnston
- The Body Keeps the Score: Brain, Mind, and Body in the Healing of Trauma by Bessell van der Kol

Best "How To" Books & Guides

- The Easiest Way to Control Alcohol by Allen Carr
- Not Drinking Tonight: A Guide to Creating a Sober Life You Love by

Amanda E. White
- Tired of Thinking about Drinking: Take My 100 Day Sober Challenge by Belle Roberson

# 14

## WHAT IS DETOXIFICATION?

(Commonly referred to as Detox) is often the first step in addiction treatment plans, especially for certain substances such as alcohol or heroin. Detox is the process of your body ridding itself of drugs or alcohol when you decide to discontinue the substance. It's very vital to get professional help.
Detoxification can purge the liver, the kidneys, and ingestion of harmful toxins.

Detoxing from alcohol or drugs involves removing toxic substances from your body while managing withdrawal symptoms that occur simultaneously. Detoxing typically takes three to ten days. However, a more severe addiction can extend detox by several weeks or even months.

Some people like to do "cold turkey ". An abrupt stop is dangerous. Most experts caution against the cold turkey approach. They suggest tapering, or slowly weaning off the drug under a doctor's supervision.

# 15

# 12 STEP PROGRAMS

The 12 steps in AA are:

- Step 1: Admit that your life has become unmanageable
- Step 2: Accept that you need God to become sober
- Step 3: Decide to turn your life over to God
- Step 4: Honestly take stock of your life
- Step 5: Admit your wrongs to yourself, God and others
- Step 6: Be ready to have God remove your character defects
- Step 7: Ask God to remove your shortcomings
- Step 8: Write down everyone you've harmed during your addiction and be ready to make amends
- Step 9: Make amends to those you've harmed
- Step 10: Continue to honestly look at your actions and admit when you are wrong
- Step 11: Pray to God for direction and the power to follow those directions

- Step 12: Put into practice what you've learned and carry the message of faith and recovery to other addicts

    It's a lot of surrendering, Letting go and Letting God.

# 16

# SETTING RECOVERY GOALS

How to set goals the SMART way

When creating goals use the acronym SMART:

- **S**pecific: Rather than setting vague goals ( ex: stay strong in recovery), be specific. Choose actions that you know will help with sobriety, like going to counseling sessions on time every week or finding a new job that will be less stressful and more fulfilling. Write down your goal: studies show that a person who writes down their goals is 33 percent more likely to achieve them.

- **M**easurable: How can you measure the success of your goals? For example, you might want to send out ten resumes this month, attend 3 recovery group meetings a week, etc. When you can measure your success, you feel good about your achievement and motivated to keep going.

**A**ttainable: If you set a goal that will be too hard to realistically achieve, you will only get discouraged. To set attainable goals, you need to know yourself. If you have never run a mile in your life, don't set a goal to run a marathon the next day. Instead set small goals that you can increase incrementally. Also, don't set a goal that depends on another person's participation. For example: "heal my marriage" isn't necessarily an attainable goal if your partner isn't on board. Instead you could set a goal to work with a therapist to learn about your role and how to find peace within yourself.

**R**ealistic: Realistic goals are critical. While it may be possible for you to stop smoking this year, is it realistic? If you're new to recovery, maybe it is not a realistic goal for you to quit smoking until you are more stable in your recovery. Instead, you could set a goal to smoke 20% less than you currently do. Eventually you will be able to quit altogether, but there is no need to add pressure until you are ready to handle it.

**T**imely: Set a goal that has a time frame. How long will it take you to complete this goal? Keep this time limit short., maybe 1-3 months. Putting a time limit on your goal will keep you focused and motivated to push forward. At the end of the time frame, you can reevaluate and set another goal.

## National Helplines

1-800-662-4357
It's the Substance abuse and Mental Health Services (SAMHSA)

It is a free, confidential, 24/7, 365-day-a-year treatment referral and information service.

# 17

# BUILDING A SUPPORT SYSTEM

5 Steps to building a Solid Support System During Addiction

- Don't be afraid to ask for help
- Determine what you want from your support and get rid of any baggage
- Attend regular recovery and support meetings
- Don't get into any new relationships or life-altering careers
- Be patient and allow time to run its course.

**Celebrate Recovery**

What it is is a Christ-centered program that provides care and support to people struggling with addiction and other life issues. The program is based on the teachings of Jesus Christ, and the goal is to help people find hope, healing, and freedom from their destructive problems.

One of the most important parts of recovery is to find you a sponsor. They will walk you through your journey. They are usually a phone call away and will meet with you regularly to aid you in your recovery.

# 18

# BIBLE STUDY GROUPS

Some people don't want to do AA or other programs and then some want to add to the AA program with a group of their peers in a bible study group. You have to find what works for you and leads you to the road to recovery. A Lot of churches have programs to help with addiction.

# 19

# CONCLUSION

I wish you the very best on your journey, be patient with yourself, I did not start to see the miracles coming for about a year. There's a saying "that the good news is you get your feelings back and the bad news is you get your feelings back."
I strongly urge you **NOT** to get into a new relationship for at least a year.
Your brain is healing, you are **not** thinking straight.
Get a sponsor, go to meetings even if you don't want to, that's usually when you need them the most, get involved, talk to others in your group.
Pray daily.

Please if you would be so kind as to leave a favorable review on Amazon for my book I would be so grateful.

Most of all, God Bless you
Melodie

# 20

# RESOURCES

*Healthline: Medical information and health advice you can trust.* (n.d.). Healthline. https://www.healthline.com/

Laranjeira, R., & Mitsuhiro, S. S. (2011b). Addiction Research Centres and the Nurturing of Creativity. National Institute on Alcohol and Drugs Policies, Brazil. *Addiction, 107*(4), 727–732. https://doi.org/10.1111/j.1360-0443.2011.03380.x

*MentalHealth.org - Your one-stop access to Mental Health.* (n.d.-a). https://www.mentalhealth.org/

*Have a problem with alcohol? There is a solution. | Alcoholics Anonymous.* (n.d.). https://aa.org/

## About the Author

Welcome, I'm a proud mom of four, a grandmother of 8 and one more coming in December. I live in Brentwood, Tennessee, I do hope this book helps you on your journey to recovery.

Made in the USA
Las Vegas, NV
20 November 2023